Animal Habitats

The Hummingbird in the Flowers

Text by Susan Quimby Foster

Photographs by Wendy Shattil and Bob Rozinski/ Oxford Scientific Films

**Gareth Stevens Publishing
Milwaukee**

Contents

The whirring of wings	3	Nesting and laying eggs	20
The hummingbird's body	4	Baby birds in the nest	22
Jewels in the sky	8	Friends and neighbors	24
Living helicopters	10	Predators and other dangers	26
Hummingbird flowers	12	Hummingbirds and people	28
The hummingbird's appetite	14	Life among the flowers	30
The long-distance travelers	16	Glossary and Index	32
Claiming a territory	18		

Note: The use of a capital letter for a hummingbird's name indicates that it is a *species* of hummingbird (for example, Rufous Hummingbird). The use of a lowercase, or small, letter means that it is a member of a larger *group* of hummingbirds.

Members of the large hummingbird family range from the tip of South America to southern Alaska.

Hummingbirds live wherever wildflowers bloom — near water, and in deserts, forests, plains, and mountains.

The whirring of wings

Even before you see a hummingbird, you will probably hear the humming sound it makes as it flies. A hummingbird can hover in the air and dart forward and backward with equal skill. The wings beat so fast that they seem invisible. As it moves, the small tapered body flashes in the sunlight, almost like a neon sign. When it feeds, the needle-shaped bill and long tongue probe deep into flowers in search of *nectar*.

Hummingbirds are some of the smallest birds in the world. They range from the size of a large bee (the Cuban Bee Hummingbird) to the length of a starling (the Giant Hummingbird of South America). Although they appear frail, hummingbirds are tough little birds. Some live 15,000 feet (5,000 m) high in the Andes Mountains of Peru. All hummingbirds are energetic, bold, and curious.

There are about 320 *species* of birds in the large hummingbird family, and they all live in North and South America. They range from Tierra del Fuego, at the southern tip of South America, all the way north into southern Alaska. The Anna's Hummingbird and a subspecies of the Allen's Hummingbird remain along the west coast of North America all year long. But most hummingbirds live throughout the year in the tropical rain forests and mountains of Ecuador and Colombia. Each spring, 21 species travel from the Central and South American tropics to North America. They make their summer homes near streams and in *evergreen* forests, areas near streams, deserts, plains, and mountains. They are found wherever wildflowers bloom, as these provide the birds with nectar, their most important food.

Hummingbirds require more food energy than any other bird.

The hummingbird's body

Streamlined form and shining metallic color are the hummingbird's specialty. The males of a few species bear remarkable plumage, including decorative crests, whiskers, and streaming tail feathers. Many display a colorful patch of feathers on the throat, called a *gorget*. As their names imply, such South American hummingbirds as the Wire-crested Thorntail, Booted Racket-tail, Horned Sungem, and Green-tailed Trainbearer are adorned with showy feathers. Females are inconspicuous, as is fitting for a bird that sits for long periods on a nest.

All hummingbirds have tiny feet that they use to perch and to comb their feathers. The birds are rarely seen landing on the ground, and their feet are ineffective for walking or hopping about. When moving farther than just a few inches, hummingbirds take to the air.

Hummingbirds can feed only on flowers that suit their beaks in shape and length. As a result, this family of birds displays a remarkable variety of beak types. The Sword-billed's beak is like a pair of flying forceps. Its four-inch- (10-cm-) long bill is the perfect eating utensil for probing into large, hanging Datura blossoms. Some hummingbirds have curved beaks. The White-tipped Sicklebill slips its beak easily into the curved flowers of a wild plantain. Nectar deep inside the South American scarlet passionflower is a perfect match for the beak of the Long-tailed Hermit. Flowers with wider and shallower shapes, meanwhile, are a free-for-all to nectar-seekers with less specialized beaks.

A hummingbird's tongue is wonderfully designed for reaching nectar. It is very long, forked, and fringed at the tip. A hummingbird can stretch out its tongue to twice the length of its bill. But the tongue does not draw up nectar like a straw. Nectar is sponged up by the tip of the tongue. It is then drawn into the mouth at a lickety-split rate of 13 licks per second.

Hummingbirds may be as small as your thumb or as large as a starling.

A hummingbird's beak is perfectly shaped to reach deep into flowers for nectar.

The humming sound that hummingbirds make comes from the vibration of their wings. As they beat their wings, the wind passes through notches in the feathers. But hummingbirds also make noises from the voice box in their throats. The West Indies' Vervain Hummingbird, which lives in dark rain forests, is a drab little bird that communicates with many attractive sounds. It seems to have substituted song for showy feathers. Most North American species are capable of little more than pleasant, high-pitched twittering. Hummingbirds have a keen sense of hearing, but color display is their primary means of communication.

    Hummingbirds have very strong pectoral muscles. These muscles are attached to the breastbone. They give the bird its power to fly. In hummingbirds, one part of the pectoral muscles pulls the wings up, and another part pulls them down. This happens very rapidly and with great force. In fact, hummingbirds' wings beat so rapidly that we usually see nothing more than a blur. The wing movement is best seen by using slow-motion photography.

A hummingbird needs large amounts of energy to fuel its active body. Like all warm-blooded animals, it must work hard to keep a constant body temperature. This process is complicated by the bird's small size. The smaller the animal, the larger its surface area is in relation to its bulk. This means that small animals lose heat rapidly when the weather is cold, and heat up fast when it is hot. The Cuban Bee Hummingbird, weighing less than 1/15th ounce (2 g), is probably as small as a bird can be without dying of starvation, no matter how fast or how much it eats. Hummingbirds are able to stave off hunger for short periods of time by storing small amounts of food in a part of their digestive system called the crop.

All living things produce heat. Hummingbirds use some of this heat to maintain their body temperature at between 104° and 110°F (40° to 43°C). In hot weather, hummingbirds cool themselves by panting like a dog. On cold nights, their lives are threatened because they have no insulating downy feathers. Severe weather may also prevent them from finding food.

Easily digested flower nectars are a ready source of food for the insatiable hummingbird.

Jewels in the sky

Male hummingbirds are among the showiest birds in the world. Their feathers glisten and shimmer as though decked out in emeralds, rubies, and amethysts. Although no less important than males, females are generally drab and secretive as they flutter and dart about. The Magnificent, Ruby-throated, Cuban Emerald, and Violet-crowned Hummingbirds are just a few of the species whose names are inspired by their beauty. Surprisingly, however, hummingbird feathers contain only black and reddish brown *pigments*. All other colors, from sparkling red to elegant deep violet, are caused by the interaction of light with the surface of the feather.

    The central shaft of every feather branches out into many hundreds of slender barbs on each side. Projecting from each barb are two opposite rows of even more minute barbules. At the tip of the barbules are microscopic hooks called barbicels. When a hummingbird *preens* its feathers, it uses its beak and claws to link the barbules together by the barbicels. In this way, unruly feathers are tamed and smoothed into silky elegance.

    Feathers on the gorgets and crowns of male hummingbirds are even more intricately designed. The top third of each barbule is flattened and has no hooklike barbicels. This region is packed with eight to ten layers of bubble-filled structures called *platelets*. When light passes through a platelet, it is bent in such a way as to give off many colors. The colors we see on the hummingbird depend on two things: the thickness of the platelets and the size of the air bubbles inside them.

Hummingbirds are among the most brilliantly colored animals in the world.

In direct sunlight, the gorget of a male Broadtailed Hummingbird seems to sparkle with red color.

The gorget is subdued when the light changes on those feathers.

As you watch a hummingbird, you will see the feathers flash with colors that change as the bird moves. This iridescence is created by the flattened barbules. They reflect colors created by the platelets just as a mirror would. The color we see depends upon the position of the bird in relation to our eyes and the Sun. When in the shadow, barbules reflect no light at all and the gorget appears black. In the sunlight, feathers of the gorget create a continuous iridescent surface because they overlap like little scales. The more consistent color on the bird's back is due to feather structure, too. In this area, barbules curve inward like *concave* mirrors. They disperse light much less dramatically in all directions.

The sparkling effect on this bird's gorget is caused by light reflecting from minute mirrors in each feather.

This Rufous Hummingbird is held in midair by wings beating between 38 and 78 times per second.

Living helicopters

Birds can fly because of the design and shape of their wings. Humans often envy birds for their ability to fly. Each wing is *convex* above and concave below. On each wing beat, air moves more rapidly over the top of the wing than over its lower surface. The effect is to lift the bird into the air. But the hummingbird is unequaled by other birds as the acrobat of the skies. As you might guess, it has much to do with its specialized wing structure.

The wings of a hummingbird are supported by long finger bones that extend into the tapered wing tips. The bones of the upper and lower arm are short and joined rigidly together at the wrist and elbow. This makes them stiff, unlike the wings of other birds. The shoulder joint is remarkably flexible. It allows the wing to turn over completely on each wing beat. This movement works in the same way as the oars on a boat that pivot in your hands as you row.

A hummingbird changes direction by pivoting its wings and tilting its body in different planes.

Hovering　　　Forward　　　Upward　　　Backward

Because the wings can twist around like this, they are able to lift and propel the bird forward on both the upstroke and the downstroke. Hummingbird flight is further controlled by the tilting and fanning out of the tail feathers.

The tiny wing tips of a hovering hummingbird trace small figure-eight patterns in the air. The bird can move forward or backward out of a hover. It simply tilts its wings and body slightly forward or backward. Now, the wings trace little ovals in the air. A small hummingbird is kept airborne by beating its wings between 38 and 78 times per second. By comparison, a vulture beats its wings only once per second, while a raven is kept aloft by flapping its wings 3.6 times per second.

No other bird can accelerate instantly from a hover to full speed. A frightened bird can even flip over backward and fly off upside down! These surprising feats give the impression that hummingbirds fly at high speeds. This is just an illusion resulting from their small size. In truth, hummingbirds usually fly no faster than most songbirds, averaging 25-30 mph (40-48 kph). The record for a hummingbird is held by a Violet-eared Hummingbird clocked at 56 mph (90 kph). However, this can't compare with the amazing speed of the Peregrine Falcon, the fastest bird known, which reaches over 200 mph (320 kph) in a dive. Swifts soar with ease at 100 mph (160 kph).

A Broadtailed Hummingbird's wings move in figure-eight patterns as the bird hovers at a flower.

Wings tracing tiny ovals in the air guide this Hermit Hummingbird forward to a flower.

Hummingbirds feed voraciously when penstemons and other wildflowers are in bloom.

The red and orange tubular flowers of the Ocotillo are especially attractive to hummingbirds in the deserts of the southwestern United States.

Hummingbird flowers

Hummingbirds feed only from certain kinds of flowers. These special hummingbird flowers are often red and attract the birds with showy blossoms. A long, tubular petal ensures that the sweet nectar inside is well beyond the reach of butterfly tongues and burrowing bees. In fact, honeybees prefer flowers with stronger perfumes. Hummingbird flowers have no flat petals for insects like bees to land on. Hummingbirds, of course, don't need to land; they hover while they feed.

Hummingbirds and their flowers are made for each other. The bird's slender head, long beak, and extendable tongue can reach deep inside the blossom. Widely spaced flowers provide ample room for hovering wings, and thick petals protect them from damage from vigorous poking and probing. Hummingbirds can feed from the same flower again and again. The flowers produce huge amounts of nectar that is replaced almost as soon as it is eaten. Some nectars contain antibiotics that help protect the birds from disease.

Nectar is about one-quarter sugar. It is a valuable food that provides energy for hummingbirds. Why have flowers given hummingbirds such a gift of high-energy food? It is an astounding fact that many plants could not make seeds if it were not for hummingbirds. The birds help the flowers make seeds by carrying *pollen* from one flower to another of the same species. This is called *pollination*. It is only after a flower has been pollinated that its seeds can grow.

 Because their survival depends upon it, hummingbird flowers have developed clever ways to coat any visiting birds with pollen. Hummingbirds cannot reach nectar without rubbing their heads against a pollen-producing structure called the *anther*. Clusters of these male flower parts are conveniently arranged at the blossom's opening. The hummingbird, unknowingly dusted with golden pollen, flies off to find more nectar.

 The flowers become pollinated when the bird transfers its burden of pollen to the *pistil* of another flower. The pistil is the female flower part. Pollen on a visiting bird easily sticks to the tip of the pistil, which pokes out of the blossom. From here each pollen grain sprouts a little tube that penetrates down the length of the pistil to a swelling near its base. This swelling is the *ovary,* where the flower's eggs are housed. Each pollen tube actually enters an egg and fertilizes it. The fertilized eggs can now grow into seeds. As they grow, the seeds are protected inside the ovary. Later in the year, the seeds will be scattered. Some may grow into new flowers that will provide nectar for more hummingbirds.

Hovering safely above dangerous spines, a bird extracts nectar, pollen, and insects from the flower of a Claret Cup Cactus.

The Anna's Hummingbird feeds from over 1,000 flowers each day.

The hummingbird's appetite

As you might suspect, hummingbirds burn up lots of energy and so they are always hungry. They spend most of their time searching for food. An Anna's Hummingbird visits over 1,000 fuchsia flowers each day to obtain enough energy to survive through the night. Nectar is their main source of energy. It provides them with water, sugar, fats, vitamins, and minerals. A hummingbird consumes half its body weight in sugar each day.

But hummingbirds do not feed on nectar alone. They are *omnivores* and need to eat animal proteins. They catch and eat insects by swiping them from the air or plucking them from spiderwebs, flowers, leaves, and other surfaces. Some hummingbirds eat other foods, too. Four North American species lap tree sap from holes made by birds known as Yellow-bellied Sapsuckers. A few South American species drink honeydew, which is a sweet secretion produced by some insects. Hummingbirds are sometimes seen sipping juices from fruits and berries.

A hummingbird flower provides a visitor with water, sugar, vitamins, and minerals.

Nectar deep at the base of the passionflower is reached only by the Long-tailed Hermit's tapered beak.

All animals need to breathe oxygen. The oxygen is used to change sugar into a form of energy useful to the body. The hummingbird's need for energy is so great that it consumes oxygen faster than any other known animal. A perching hummingbird breathes at a rate of 250 times per minute (humans breathe at a rate of about 17 times per minute when at rest). But this rate increases by seven times when the bird takes to the air.

Sugar and oxygen are carried by the blood to every part of the little bird's body. Pumping the blood along is the largest heart known in the animal kingdom, relative to overall body size. It beats at a rate of 500 times per minute in a resting bird and accelerates to 1,200 beats per minute when the bird is active.

Curiosity and a highly developed sense of color vision help young birds find food by trial and error. At first, a red handkerchief and a flower are of equal interest. But they soon discover that only the flowers promise a reward of nectar. The birds learn not just flowers' shapes and colors, but which ones produce the most and the sweetest nectars. Hummingbirds will return to a good feeding place year after year. They are very protective of the flowers growing in their home territory. They discourage thieves by removing nectar from flowers at the edge of their domains before feeding from flowers in the interior.

Traveling a round trip from Central America to Alaska each year, the tiny Rufous Hummingbird migrates 2,500 miles (4,000 km) each way.

The long-distance travelers

The vast majority of hummingbirds stay all year in the rain forests of South and Central America. The 21 species that migrate to North America experience less competition from other hummingbirds for their preferred breeding sites and foods. They escape the harsh winters by traveling south each autumn. It is likely that many of the hummingbird flowers of North America came into being in association with hummingbirds in the tropics long ago. But as the birds established their migration routes, these flowering plants followed them. Over thousands of years, the plants have become more and more dependent on either one or a few hummingbird species for pollination.

Every spring seven species of hummingbirds travel north to the Rocky Mountains to breed. Four other species migrate as far as Canada. The adventurous Rufous Hummingbird reaches as far as Alaska. Only the Ruby-throat moves from the tropics to the plains and hills east of the Mississippi. It is amazing how far some of these tiny birds can travel. Twice a year, the

Ruby-throated Hummingbird flies for 26 hours nonstop. It covers more than 500 miles (800 km) across the Gulf of Mexico. The Rufous Hummingbird, no larger than your thumb, must cover the 2,500 miles (4,000 km) between Central America and Alaska each autumn and spring.

Migration can be full of danger for these bold little birds. But hummingbirds have a way of storing energy needed for a long migration. They keep energy on reserve as fat inside the liver and beneath the skin. Before migration, Ruby-throated Hummingbirds gain roughly half of their body weight in fat storage. Birds living high in the mountains often keep very large stores of fat in their livers.

Hummingbirds have a memory for reliable food sources and return to them year after year.

In springtime and early summer, hummingbirds perch only briefly to rest.

Female Broadtailed Hummingbirds enter the male's territory to feed, and quickly fly away.

Claiming a territory

Hummingbird males and females come together briefly, solely for the purpose of mating. Males are masters of self-advertisement, perhaps out of a need to attract a mate when the environment is best suited for the females to raise a family. In the dark tropical rain forests of Guyana, up to a hundred drab male Long-tailed Hermits congregate and announce themselves by singing. Mating of tropical hummingbirds takes place all year round, but each species tends to confine its activities to a specific season.

The whistling buzz of a hummingbird in May is a sure sign that spring has come to the Rocky Mountains. Male Broadtailed Hummingbirds are the first to arrive from Central America, appearing only one at a time. In a few weeks, they crowd noisily around flowers and bird feeders. No sooner has one hungry bird hovered to drink nectar than another fiercely chases it away. These tiny green rivals are fighting for a good source of nectar. They dart and somersault through the air until one declares himself the winner. In this quarrelsome, unfriendly fashion, a male hummingbird becomes the owner of a feeding territory.

A male Broadtailed Hummingbird protects his territory from all intruders, including wasps, butterflies, and birds as well as people. He declares ownership by showing off the glittering, ruby red gorget feathers beneath his chin. He also performs a hair-raising flying show called an *aerial display*. The display begins when he climbs steeply into the air above his food source. He hovers several times as he rises in the ascent to be sure that he is noticed by all below. Emitting a shrill screech, he suddenly plummets headfirst toward the ground. The dive is broken just a few feet from certain death. The bird then veers off to the side to check the security of his territory. These aerial displays are repeated many times during the day. If you are wearing red, a diving bird may zoom like a missile past your ears or stop to hover inquisitively right before your nose — thinking that you are a flower!

Female Broadtails migrate north slightly later than the males. Their backs are shimmering olive green, and their breasts are cream, mottled with brown. Their wings give out only a hushed murmur. They dart into defended territories to feed and then quickly whir away. Males try to attract them by flashing their brilliant colors and dancing zigzags in the air. Their gorgets seem ablaze in the sunlight. Fleeing females are pursued into shrubbery, where males attempt to mate with them. Male and female hummingbirds usually live apart. The only time the two sexes spend together is when they mate.

Following spring migration, Broadtailed Hummingbirds establish and fiercely defend their food sources.

The Broadtailed Hummingbird's nest is a cozy collection of cobwebs, lichens, and other materials molded by the mother bird's beak and body.

Nesting and laying eggs

Year-round breeding activity is reported for Anna's and Allen's Hummingbirds in California and the Andean Hillstar of Ecuador. But even in tropical areas, the little birds tend to confine this activity to the season in which the preferred flowers bloom. It is no accident that the breeding season of North American hummingbirds is in late spring and early summer. At that time of year there is an abundance of flowers, mosquitoes, gnats, and mites. An excess of food increases the chance that the birds will survive to mate. It also sustains the females through the hardships of nesting and raising babies. While other birds are luring mates with song, male hummingbirds are fiercely defending their territories. The females quietly select good nesting sites close by.

The hummingbird's nest is a miraculous concoction of cobwebs, seed silks, insect cocoons, pine needles, and lichens. The female hummingbird fastens these materials securely to tree limbs, leaves, or vines with sticky spiderwebs. She weaves fibers together using her beak and claws. Finally, she pats her feet on the bottom of the nest and presses her breast against its rim. In this way, she shapes the nest into a deep cup.

The tiny hummingbird nest blends so well with branches and leaves that it is very difficult to see.

The common chicken egg is immense in comparison to a hummingbird egg.

When it is finished, the nest opening is barely two inches (5 cm) wide. It is soft on the inside, but outside it is durable and waterproof. Hummingbird nests are hard to see against tree bark and leaves. The Hermit Hummingbird of South America fastens its nest beneath the leaf that shelters it from the rain. The Broadtailed Hummingbird, nesting in North America, cleverly hides its nest among vegetation on a branch sometimes only four feet (1.2 m) above the ground.

The body of a female hummingbird is amazingly efficient. A single egg can weigh as much as 20 percent of her total body weight. It is more common for an egg to make up only 2 to 4 percent of a mother bird's weight. Despite its large size in relation to the mother's body, the hummingbird's egg is the smallest known in the bird world. It is white, oval, less than 1/2 inch (1.2 cm) long, and weighs only 0.018 ounce (0.5 g). Two eggs are laid, usually two days apart. If baby birds are to develop, the eggs must be incubated. The female warms them by nestling her breast against them. Heat is released from a specialized area of her breast that is rich in blood vessels. The expectant mother incubates her eggs for up to 80 percent of each day and keeps them at about 90°F (32°C). Each developing baby is nourished by a nutrient-rich yolk inside the egg. Oxygen and other gases pass freely through small pores in the eggshell.

A mother hummingbird lays two eggs in her nest and incubates them for 15 to 22 days.

Two baby Broadtailed Hummingbirds huddle together for warmth while their mother is in search of food.

Baby birds gape in eager anticipation of their mother's regurgitated nectar and insects.

Baby birds in the nest

After 15 to 22 days, the baby chicks hatch. Helped by strong neck muscles and a chisel-like tooth on the beak, each baby bird taps the inside of the shell until it cracks open. Their tidy mother removes bits of shell from the nest to prevent predators from finding her babies. Later she will also remove their droppings from the nest to keep it clean. The chicks are naked, blind, and helpless when they first hatch. The mother snuggles and warms her babies by *brooding* them. At night, the cozy nest protects mother and babies from the cold.

The father plays no part in rearing the chicks. But the mother is busy indeed! She protects her young from any predators that try to plunder the nest for food. Common threats to babies include hawks, crows, chipmunks, jays, and snakes. When not brooding, the mother flies about in search of food. She feeds her youngsters about one to three times an hour throughout the day. The little begging chicks gape open their red-lined mouths the instant their mother returns. She feeds them by *regurgitating* a mixture of nectar and insects she has stored in her crop.

At one to two weeks after hatching, the chicks are covered with new feathers. The feathers come through the skin enclosed in delicate sheaths that burst open as they dry. Once the feathers are dry and fully expanded, the chicks can keep themselves warm. The brooding period is over. On each wing there are ten long primary feathers. Ten new tail feathers will soon be in use to help the young hummingbird steer, balance, and brake when it is flying.

The little birds stretch their wings often and exercise their long tongues. At about twenty-one days of age, they suddenly take flight. Their first landings are clumsy, but their flying skills improve. Their bold nature leads them to explore many natural foods. Soon they are showering in lawn sprinklers and splashing in waterfalls. They receive the last meal from their mother when they are about a month and a half old. Then they are ready to find their own food from the hummingbird flowers.

At about three weeks of age, the babies take to the air with little more practice than wing exercises.

Wasps, butterflies, ants, and bees share the hummingbird's thirst for nectar.

Hummingbirds and bees do plants a great service by transferring pollen from one flower to another.

Friends and neighbors

Hummingbirds share their thirst for nectar with many other animals. Some bees are known to chew their way through petals to reach the honey pot at the base of a flower. Several birds pierce holes in flowers using their beaks. Butterflies and ants love nectar, too.

Hummingbirds have a curious relationship with a group of tiny animals called mites. These creatures live and breed inside hummingbird flowers where they, too, feed on nectar. As many as twelve mites may jump aboard a feeding hummingbird and hide in its nostrils. After hitching a ride to the next flower, they scoot down the bird's bill to the petals. The hummingbird serves as an airliner, carrying the mites to new supplies of food.

Each spring, North American gardeners, bird watchers, photographers, and many others eagerly await the return of the hummingbirds. At the first sound of their buzzing wings, people hang out their hummingbird feeders, hoping that a male will select their garden as his territory. The feeders allow us to watch the dazzling little birds at close range, just beyond the windowpane or next to a favorite picnic spot. We watch cats, larger birds, butterflies, bees, and wasps backing away from these aggressive little birds. It is amusing to find that hummingbirds are upset when people approach to refill a feeder.

The sticky silk of a spider's web is an ideal building material for a hummingbird nest.

People in North America can easily make hummingbirds their neighbors by planting hummingbird flowers such as columbines, penstemons, and larkspurs in their gardens. And they can hang up a feeding bottle in a place that is safe from cats and other dangers! A mixture of sugar and water will help attract hummingbirds.

In late summer, the hummingbirds will gorge themselves on nectar. This is how they build fat reserves needed for migration. The feeder should be left in place until the last hummingbird has gone. The hummingbirds know exactly when they should migrate to a warmer climate.

A gray squirrel manages to steal some sugar water from a hummingbird feeder.

Capable of outmaneuvering predators most of the time, hummingbirds are an occasional meal for the American Kestrel.

Predators and other dangers

Most hummingbirds can escape any animal that tries to catch them. Even so, they must always be on the alert for predators such as American Kestrels, Pigeon Hawks, Roadrunners, and orioles. Occasionally, a Leopard Frog or a fish will jump out of the water to snatch a hovering bird from the air. Some hummingbirds are even tiny enough to be taken by a dragonfly while both are on the wing! Small hummingbirds make a meal for a patient spider or praying mantis. It is not uncommon for a domestic cat to intercept a hummingbird as it flies between perch and bird feeder.

Hummingbirds may also become the victims of other disasters. The spines of thistles and foxtail grass needles may snare them. Mistaking their own reflection in glass for an invading male, they may die from colliding with windowpanes. They are also occasionally found with their beaks stuck in finely meshed window screens. Some are poisoned by chemicals like DDT, which are used to kill insect pests. Although now outlawed in the United States, poisonous DDT is still used to control insects in other countries.

The toxin enters birds through their insect foods and collects in their bodies. Birds poisoned by DDT produce eggs with very weak shells, and cracked shells will never protect birds so they can develop properly.

Hummingbirds suffer badly from the cold; severe weather and cold nights can kill them. Hummingbirds can survive these hard times by passing into *torpor*. In torpor, a bird requires only 1/50th of its normal demand for energy. Breathing and heart rates are drastically lowered, and it is not uncommon for a torpid bird to pass extended periods of time without breathing at all. Body temperatures may drop as much as 68°F (20°C). When dawn or good weather returns, the birds slowly return to normal. You may be surprised some day to come across a torpid bird, but it should not be disturbed. Although it seems lifeless, it may become alert and suddenly fly away.

The acrobatic hummingbird is no match for a Peregrine Falcon, which reaches 200 miles per hour (320 kph) in a dive.

This hummingbird mask may help the Apache dancer feel closer to the supernatural world.

A modern American Indian artist, Robert Sebastian, captures the essence of a hummingbird in a silk screen.

Hummingbirds and people

Hummingbirds have been admired by native peoples of Central and South America for thousands of years. The Aztecs used hummingbirds and their feathers to adorn their ceremonial cloaks. The birds were placed in the tombs of warriors, and medicine men wore them around their necks. They were believed to possess magical powers.

Europeans knew nothing about hummingbirds until 1558. In that year a French explorer reported seeing them in the New World. Europeans were understandably impressed by the beauty of these exotic little birds. They wanted specimens to study, admire, and display. Sadly, some people saw a chance to make money out of these birds. They started to market hummingbird specimens and products abroad. American Indians captured wild hummingbirds to meet the foreign demand. In 1888 alone, 400,000 skins of hummingbirds and other North and South American birds were sold in London markets. Their feathers decorated the fans, necklaces, and bonnets of stylish ladies. Also, thousands of birds were sold during the late 1800s to zoos, museums, and private collections around the world.

It is fortunate for hummingbirds that fashions and attitudes changed. In 1900, the United States took sweeping action to protect hummingbirds and other endangered wildlife. The Lacey Act, updated in 1981, prohibits the import, export, transport, sale, or purchase of wild animals and plants. The Migratory Bird Act of 1918 protects game and nongame birds. More recently, South American countries such as Ecuador and Brazil have also passed laws to protect wildlife.

Many people around the world are concerned about the practice of burning and clearing tropical rain forests. In these forests is the habitat of the majority of hummingbird species. If the present destruction of the rain forests continues, some hummingbirds and countless other living things may become extinct. This means that they will disappear forever from the face of the Earth. Many governments and conservation organizations see this problem as an emergency. They are working to save the remaining rain forests. Through their efforts, your grandchildren may live to enjoy hummingbirds tomorrow as much as you do today.

Hopi Indians of Arizona carved kachinas in the likeness of hummingbirds for use in their ceremonies.

Life among the flowers

Hummingbirds share their habitat with many other plants and animals. These living things and their nonliving environment are closely interrelated to form an ecosystem. Plants use energy from sunlight to make sugars out of water and carbon dioxide. The sugar is changed into important building materials in the plant's leaves, stems, roots, and flowers.

Many insects, birds, and mammals rely on plants for food. These animals, in turn, are meals for predators. Hummingbirds are a part of such a food chain. They obtain sugar directly from flower nectar and protein by eating insects. The hummingbird predator, be it American Kestrel or Leopard Frog, may be eaten by the Great Horned Owl or another predator. When plants and animals die, the nutrients in their bodies return to the soil through the process of decomposition.

Food chain

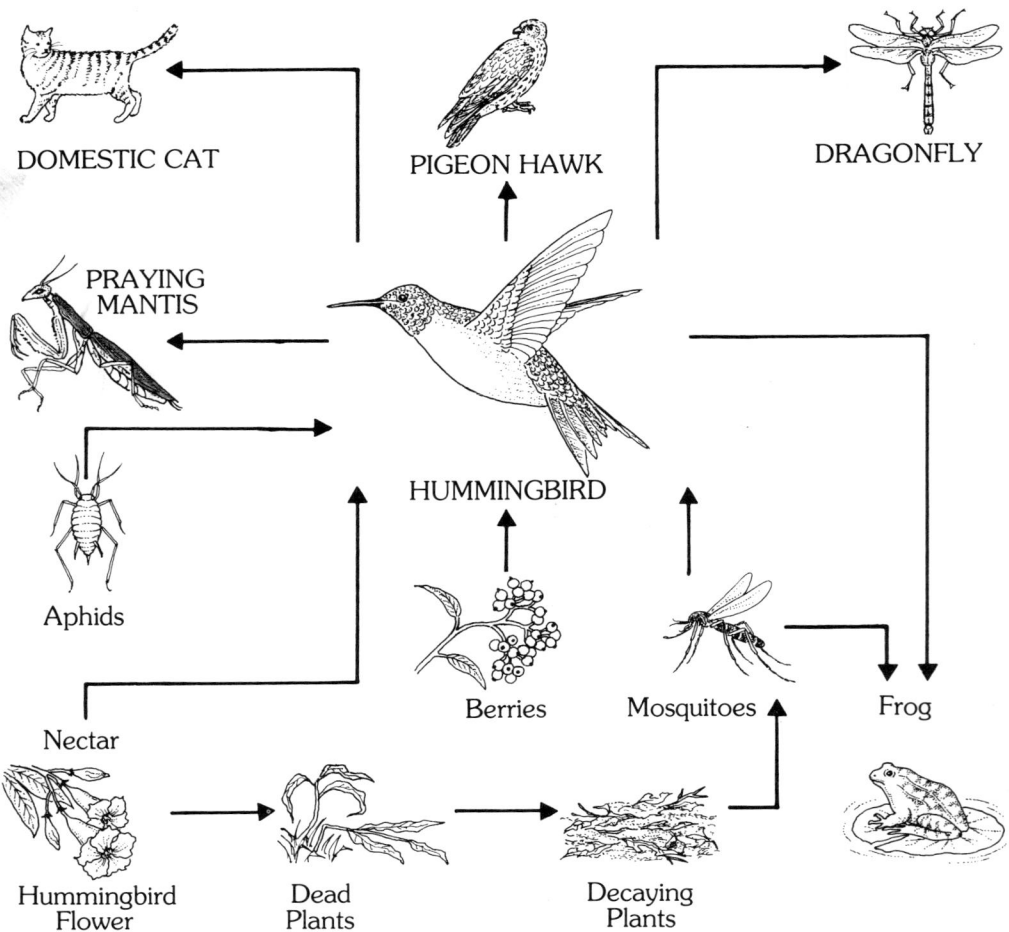

The aerial acrobatics and shimmering color of a hummingbird are a delight to observe.

Barring accidents, hummingbirds may live for ten years in the wild. During this time they provide an irreplaceable service to many plants in their ecosystem. For example, in the southwestern United States, 129 species of flowering plants depend upon hummingbirds for pollination. The Ruby-throated Hummingbird is the only pollinator of 21 hummingbird species found in the northeastern United States. They also help thousands of animals that depend on hummingbird plants for food and shelter.

  Our knowledge about hummingbirds is growing every day. The more we know about them, the more we marvel at their special relationship with flowers and their place in the ecosystem. We are amused by their curiosity, startled by their boldness, and thrilled by their dazzling colors and wonderful flying displays. Hummingbirds enrich the lives of all who value the wonders of the natural world.

Glossary and Index

These new words about hummingbirds appear in the text on the pages shown after each definition. Each new word first appears in the text in *italics*, just as it appears here.

aerial display . a series of flight patterns performed by male hummingbirds. **19**

anther .... the male flower part that produces pollen. **13**

brooding ...... protective behavior of birds by which the young are warmed and sheltered beneath the wings and body of a parent. **22, 23**

concave .... hollowed or arched inward like the inside of a bowl. **9, 10**

convex .... arching or curving outward like the surface of a ball. **10**

gorget .... a region of colorful feathers between the beak and the belly on a male hummingbird. **4, 8, 9, 19**

nectar .... a sugary syrup secreted by some kinds of flowers. **3, 5, 6, 7, 12-15, 18, 22, 24, 25, 30**

omnivore ...... an animal that survives by eating both plants and animals. **14**

ovary .... a swelling at the base of the pistil that contains little eggs or ova. When ova are fertilized by pollen, they develop into seeds. **13**

pigment .... a substance that gives color to structures such as the feathers, skin, and beak on a bird. **8**

pistil .... a long tube extending up from the ovary of a flower. The pistil and the ovary form the female parts of a flower. **13**

platelet .... a microscopic structure in the gorget and crown feathers on male hummingbirds. **8, 9**

pollen .... a fine powder produced on a flower's anthers. **13, 24**

pollination ... the process by which pollen is transferred from the anther of one flower to the pistil of another. Pollination results in fertilization and the formation of a seed. **13, 16, 31**

preen .... to smooth the feathers. **8**

regurgitate ... to bring up undigested food from the stomach of a mother bird to feed chicks. **22**

species .... a group of living things with like features that are able to breed and produce offspring with only their own kind. **2, 3, 4, 6, 8, 14, 16, 18, 31**

torpor .... a state of lowered body function that allows hummingbirds to survive cold nights and severe weather. **27**

Reading level analysis: FRY 6, FLESCH 82 (easy), RAYGOR 6, FOG 5, SMOG 4
Library of Congress Cataloging-in-Publication Data
Foster, Susan Q.
    The hummingbird in the flowers / words by Susan Q. Foster; photographs by Oxford Scientific Films.
       p. cm. -- (Animal habitats)
    Summary: Explains and illustrates the lives of hummingbirds in their natural habitats, showing how they feed, defend themselves, and breed.
    ISBN 0-8368-0115-6
    1. Hummingbirds--Juvenile literature. [1. Hummingbirds.] I. Oxford Scientific Films. II. Title. III. Series.
QL696.A558F68   1989
598.8'99--dc20   89-31912

North American edition first published in 1990 by Gareth Stevens Children's Books, RiverCenter Building, Suite 201, 1555 North RiverCenter Drive, Milwaukee, WI 53212, USA
Text copyright © 1990 by Oxford Scientific Films. All rights reserved. No part of this book may be reproduced in any form or by any means without permission in writing from Gareth Stevens, Inc.
Conceived, designed, and produced by Belitha Press Ltd., London. Consultant Editor: Jennifer Coldrey. Art Director: Treld Bicknell. Design: Naomi Games. US Editors: Mark J. Sachner and Rhoda Irene Sherwood. Line Drawings: Lorna Turpin.

The author and publishers wish to thank the following for permission to reproduce copyright material: **Wendy Shattil and Bob Rozinski** for title page, pp. 3, 5, 7, 9 all, 10, 11 right, 12 both, 13, 14 below, 18 both, 19, 20 both, 21 both, 22 both, 23, 24 both, 25 both, 26, 27, 28 both, 29, 31, and back cover; **Oxford Scientific Films Ltd.** for p. 2 (S. R. Morris); pp. 4 and 6 (Tom Ulrich); p. 8 and front cover (Stephen Dalton); p. 14 above (Animals Animals — Alan G. Nelson); p. 15 (Michael Fogden); p. 17 (Bruce A. MacDonald). Partridge Films Ltd. for pp. 11 left (Carol Farnetti) and 16 (Richard Foster). Pages 28 both and 29 are courtesy of the Denver Museum of Natural History.

Printed in the United States of America
1 2 3 4 5 6 7 8 9 96 95 94 93 92 91 90
For a free color catalog describing Gareth Stevens' list of high-quality children's books, call 1-800-341-3569.